BEYOND CHILDHOOD:
BECOMING
AN ADULT

LOUIE DUBOIS
(AKA: THE FORMER "GREAT ONE")

Order this book online at www.trafford.com
or email orders@trafford.com

Most Trafford titles are also available at major online book retailers.

Print information available on the last page.

ISBN: 978-1-6987-1169-0 (sc)
ISBN: 978-1-6987-1171-3 (hc)
ISBN: 978-1-6987-1170-6 (e)

Library of Congress Control Number: 2022906819

Trafford rev. 04/11/2022

 www.trafford.com

North America & international
toll-free: 844-688-6899 (USA & Canada)
fax: 812 355 4082

Remembering a Childhood Worth Remembering

while Growing from a Youth to an Adult

Names have not been changed to protect the innocent, except for one name. His name has been changed to protect the "guilty." Real names and locations have been utilized in most circumstances to show one's folly on many occasions upon reaching adulthood.

To Brother MB and Brother JJ
and, of course, Emilie Louise

CONTENTS

PROLOGUE

The following are vignettes of the late 1940s through early 1970s—anecdotes of a youth/young man in years of no responsibilities, now an old man and reminiscing on the good old days of character building. While there is some social commentary, it is at a minimum.

We all have memories of growing up: being little kids and then our formal education, elementary school. We called it grammar school, then high school, and for some, college. Not everyone was fortunate for the latter. I was one of the fortunate ones. My character was molded in grammar school and, most assuredly, high school, first by the Dominican nuns and then by the Jesuits, the last named "Teachers of the Catholic Church".

We also had dreams of where we wanted to be in life when we became adults. My dreams were to be a fireman like my father, not, but always becoming a baseball player in the major leagues. To that end, I collected baseball cards (see cover picture), played "street ball" with my friends and especially older guys. Ability honed by perceived skills with my friends by utilizing what I learned from the older guys. By the time I was seventeen, I knew I was better than my guys and the older crowd, at least in baseball.

Of course, as one gets older, you realize there is more important proficiency in a multitude of situations to attain, more preparedness in work environs, and a larger acceptance of humility than becoming a professional baseball player. Character is developed by one's reaction to failure, whether in personal relationships or in earning a living to provide for a family, should one choose that vocation.

These vignettes I've written provided a crescendo to my adulthood, with a few setbacks along the way. Boring to many, I suppose. But typical to many who grew up in the lower-middle class with parents wanting their children to succeed, to be better financially than they, and to treat others as their children want to be treated. Simple but difficult at times, no doubt. I married a terrific woman and mother. I have two terrific sons. And I still go to church! As Frank Sinatra sang, "I did it My Way." Capiche?

The following short "stories" are broken down into three simple segments:

1. **The Late 1940s and the 1950s**
2. **The 1960s**
3. **The Early 1970s**

Basically, these narratives are compendious so as not to become too tedious. Hopefully, they're in chronological order as best I can recall. There are no kept diaries. Men don't keep diaries, at least not unless one intended "someday" to write a historical truism or novel. I'm not that inclined! Some of my scenarios are funny, some not so funny, and just a handful quite serious, even in today's culture. Of course, you decide for yourself.

THE LATE 1940S AND THE 1950S

THE PRINCIPAL GROWING YEARS

Doris Day and the Movies

My dear mother loved going to the movies. She, her sister, and a good friend, Libby, went to the "picture shows" when mom was a teenager into her twenties. Not as often when mom got married.

In 1949, when I was about seven years old, my mother took me to see Doris Day in *My Dream Is Yours* with Jack Carson. (Had to look it up on the Internet to get the exact title!) I really didn't understand "what was going on" but was mesmerized by the blonde in the movie, this actress being Doris Day. Beautiful voice and cheery disposition. I saw all Ms. Day's pictures in the '40s, '50s, and '60s. While mostly on TCM for the '40s and '50s, I began a lifelong attachment to Bogie, Bette Davis, and all the thespians of those years: true picture-making, not the computer-generated sci-fi of later years. The only "real" motion pictures today are predominately historical in nature.

First Airplane Trip

In 1949 or 1950, I took my first plane ride: Idlewild International Airport (now JFK) from New York (Queens) to Miami Beach with my grandmother and my Aunt Betty (my mother's relatives). Very exciting for a little boy of seven or eight years old. We stayed with my mother's best friend from Manhattan, Mrs. Harold P. Because of my knowledge of all the statistics on the reverse of my baseball cards (see picture of me

1

on this book's cover), Aunt Betty was asked to have me appear "live" on the local television station. Auntie said no. My television career ended before it started. A Navy SEAL tried to teach me how to swim (in our host's in-ground pool), but he gave up when I started to cry because it seemed hopeless, especially with all "eyes" on us. Fast forward to now, I still don't know how to swim; hence, my aversion to being on any type-sized watercraft. The return trip to NYC was on board a Stratocruiser plane with a wonderful viewing section. As it was deemed to happen, we arrived in a terrible rainstorm. Everyone thanked the cockpit/cabin crews as we disembarked. I had an exciting flight. My Uncle Pat took us home to 51st and 1st in Manhattan via his Studebaker Champion. Then about midnight, Uncle P took me to Riker's Quick Restaurant, the forerunner of McDonald's, for a hamburger and a ride on the 3rd Avenue El to the Fordham Road area in the Bronx, where I lived. Uncle P returned to Manhattan likewise.

Santa Claus and Uncle John

Until I was eight or nine years old, I too believed in Santa Claus. I did not believe in the tooth fairy because when I lost a tooth, my pillow had zero under it the next morning. But Santa usually got me what I wanted for Christmas. One time I asked Santa for a Stan Musial baseball glove that cost $10.25. Ha! Santa delivered when I found it under the Christmas tree. Another time Brother MB and I begged Santa Claus for a decent sled so that we might enjoy sleigh-riding safely on Coles Lane, a small dead-end street off Bainbridge Avenue. We got that sled too. In fact, about that time, Santa actually called me by name. I was in the bedroom of our apartment when someone called me from the bedroom window. I knew it was Santa Claus. I took a quick peek, and no one. I told my mother that I heard Santa. A year or two later, I was sitting at my father's bedroom desk, where I usually did my homework, when I needed my pencil sharpened. I opened one or two desk drawers and found a Santa costume suit tucked away at the back of the drawer. I immediately looked at the bedroom window and at the fire escape that was with every apartment in our seven-story building. I went to the window and surmised that "Santa" had called me and then moved away from the bedroom window and closer to the bathroom window, the bathroom being next to the bedroom. Had I gone to the bedroom window and checked the fire escape, I would have found dear "Old Saint Nick" by the bathroom window. I subsequently found out that it was my Godfather, Uncle John F, who impersonated Santa Claus. I stopped believing these fairy tales from that day forward, even Rudolph the red-nosed reindeer. Another phony.

Boyhood Heroes in the Sports World

As long as I can remember, I wanted most earnestly to become a major league baseball player. As such, I had sports "heroes." Other than my father, who was my first hero, my athletic warriors were Jackie Robinson (no. 42) and Stan "the Man" Musial (no. 6) in baseball, Bobby Layne (no. 22) in football, and Gordie Howe (no. 9) in hockey. While I read all the sports pages in our local newspapers, I only followed basketball when Elgin Baylor (no. 22) became a Minneapolis Laker in 1958. These were my "heroes." And the reason I was a diehard St. Louis Cardinals fan, a Detroit Lions fan, and a Detroit Red Wings fan, and a Minneapolis/Los Angeles Lakers fan. I was a "closet" Brooklyn Dodgers fan, but living in the Bronx, that was taboo! I follow these teams religiously to this day! The only autographed picture I still have (in my scrapbook) is the one sent me by Mr. Hockey, Gordie Howe. I do have autograph pictures of Ted "Teddy Baseball" Williams and the GOAT in football, Jim Brown.

Growing up in the Bronx, as I'm confident those boys living in other professional sports towns wished also, we wanted to be star athletes when we were older. Anyway, like most young men who wanted a sports life, I followed my dream and played baseball in high school and college. Unfortunately, I have a very bad right knee that I injured when I was about sixteen years of age and didn't dare to play football for fear my knee would get hurt and bye-bye baseball career. As for basketball, if I wanted to run up and down a basketball court, I would have joined a track team. As an aside, I was voted the Intramural Athlete of the Year (in my senior year) at Fordham University. Not too shabby.

Watching First TV Show—Ernie Kovacs in 1952 or 1953

The above subject is a sneak-look into the future of Louie Dubois's awe of television. Until the above timeframe, LD listened only to radio broadcasts. My favorite station was WJZ (now I think, in TV lingo, ABC), which gave me *The Lone Ranger* and *Inner Sanctum* with the creaky door. The latter scared me often, but radio let your imagination run wild, like reading a book. Anyone can watch TV, stream shows, or go to the movies, but one never fell asleep listening to the radio.

In 1952 or 1953, my father brought home our first television set: 17-inch screen with a black and white picture made by Hallicrafter. This TV set had a cable from the back of the television to your remote control while you sat on the sofa adjusting the volume (only). Of course, to change the channel, someone had to get up and "visit" the TV. When only LD and MB were watching the TV, MB was "in charge" of changing the channels. Well, the first morning I was alone with the TV, Ernie Kovacs was on. I was about ten, so excuse me if I thought this new gadget was beaming a show only for me. I turned the set off, then quickly back on trying to see if Kovacs was entertaining only me and not others. I thought that any show I watched was "off-limits" to anyone else. Dumb, but I was only a little boy.

Through the years, I got my own small television and watched Flash Gordon, old movies, all sporting events, and *The Merry Mailman*, the latter looking for Ray Heatherton's daughter, Joey. I'm sure you all remember Joey Heatherton!

Alas, now most of the television shows, broadcast and cable, are computer-inspired reality garbage, and repeats are commonplace. For example, no more *Playhouse 90*, *You Are There*, and *The Bell Telephone Hour*. Very sad.

Joe D's Baseball Bat and Charlie Keller's Batting "Helmet"

One of my mother's younger brothers, my Uncle Pat T, loved sporting events, especially horseracing and baseball. I don't know much about his enthusiasm for the former, but I am quite familiar with the latter. When I was nine or ten years old, Uncle P gave me a Joe DiMaggio baseball bat, a Charlie "King Kong" Keller batting helmet, and a baseball signed by the 1950 New York Yankees. Every one of my friends was a Yankees fan, except for me. While I professed to be a St. Louis Cardinals fan because of Stan "The Man" Musial, I was definitely "locked in" with this team when Harvey Haddix arrived in 1952. I was also a "closet" Brooklyn Dodgers rooter; as I mentioned previously, this was because of

Jackie Robinson (no. 42) and Gil Hodges (no. 14). I was fascinated with Robinson's daring play and Hodges's footwork around first base.

The "older guys" often took me to Mosholu Park off Webster Avenue in the Bronx to play some baseball, probably because I had the DiMaggio bat and a decent baseball to hit. Chuck D was the best hitter and a lefty like me. I wanted to hit a baseball like CD when I was his age. By the way, I did. As for the Joe D bat, I'd stroll up to Mosholu Park by myself and used the bat to hit small rocks and couldn't understand how the bat broke. Besides, I didn't realize I might have hurt someone walking by on Bainbridge Avenue with some of my "moon shots."

As for the Charlie Keller batting helmet, it wasn't even a helmet. It was an NYY baseball cap with stiff cardboard on either side of the hat just over the ears. Obviously, no one threw 90–100mph in those days. Maybe one or two. (Bob Feller comes to mind.) One day there were some threads hanging beneath the NY initials and the back of the hat's peak. I pulled out one thread, then another, and several others, until the peak dislodged itself, and all that was left was a CK "beanie"! What did I know? I was probably ten years old. Goodbye, Charlie "King Kong" Keller's batting helmet! (Left fielder for the Yankees, 1939–1952, with an interruption because of WW2, and the Detroit Tigers). As for the valuable baseball with Joe DiMaggio's autograph on the ball's "sweet spot," and Casey Stengel, Phil Rizzuto, Tommy Henrich, and Lew Burdette, the latter with Warren Spahn (another of my favorite pitchers), who would beat the Yankees in the 1957 World Series and lose to the Yanks the following year, 1958. I kept this treasured baseball until Uncle P's son, P Jr. was about ten; I returned it to my uncle, who I thought was surprised that I had this baseball for about thirty-five years.

Hee-Haw in Sixth Grade

I truly enjoyed going to elementary school (calling elementary school "grammar school" would be a non sequitur in today's world) and the company of many of my classmates. Most of my classmates at OLM were bright. Some were seemingly brain-dead, or maybe they just didn't care to learn as deeply as KD, EC, JD'A, Kevin G, Phil W, or I did. In any event, the difficulties I experienced in school were because of only one of my teachers: my sixth grade nun, Sister Arnold. Looking back on that time, I guess Sister A thought me too conceited for my age. My schoolwork was excellent, but she was going to "humble" me, especially in front of the other students.

This particular day, Sister A decided to play a game with five to six of us. We lined up in front of the blackboard, and this pathetic example of a Dominican nun whispered into every boy's ear a barnyard animal. We were to all, at the count of 3, yell out our depicted interpretation of this animal with a strong emotional response. Sister would then have the class pick the "winner." At the count of 3, I put my hands to my ears and shouted, "Hee-haw, hee-haw!" All the others by the blackboard were deafly silent. I made a complete jackass of myself. Oh! Sister loved that response. I was fuming internally but calmly returned to my desk. And Sister A called herself a religious person.

Another time, my Uncle PT gave me a Sheaffer Snorkel pen and pencil set. Of course, this "precious" servant of God told me that "it was too good for me" and confiscated the set. I did get it back the end of the school year and gave the pen and pencil to my eldest son, about forty-five years later. Hopefully, he still has it for my grandson as he gets older. In eighth grade, we had handwriting exercises just about every day, first with lines on the paper, then without lines. RS had to practice his capital I. Only one boy didn't practice his handwriting: LD with his Sheaffer Snorkel pen.

Many years later, when the Catholic Church did away with most nuns being clad in the religious habits they wore in Catholic schools when I was a kid, Duke D and I took our third, fourth, fifth, and seventh grade teacher, Sister Norbert, my favorite at least, to dinner at a restaurant on City Island (Bronx, New York). At the night's end, we asked for sister's living address in Wisconsin, I think. I handed Sister N a pen and paper, which she returned to me, saying, "You write it down, Louie. Your handwriting was always better than a nun's!"

I smiled and thought to myself, *Sister A, take that, you bitch!*

As it turned out, Sister N mentioned that Sister A left the Dominican Order, probably became a social worker, my opinion.

OLM and Choir Boys
Saturday Church Confession
That Collections Listing

Our Lady of Mercy was a terrific school for learning. The Dominican nuns were thoughtful and helpful in every way, except for that one nun I had in sixth grade. Three of my classmates went to Regis High School, continuing a practice of many years, before and after our graduation class of 1956. Regis in Manhattan was the "cream of the Jesuit teaching crop." As an aside, the other three Jesuit high schools in New York City during my lifetime were Fordham Prep (my school), Brooklyn Prep, and the military Jesuit high school, Xavier. Brooklyn Prep is not with us any longer. Pity.

Altar boys and choir boys were needed for the various Masses and other religious ceremonies to be celebrated at OLM, starting with third grade assignments. In our fifth grade class, there was a shortage of choir boys, so Sister N auditioned the boys to pick those she thought would be a good "fit" for "when needed." This meant every Sunday's 11:00 a.m. High Mass in addition to having to attend the regular Sunday 9:00 a.m. children's Mass held downstairs at OLM's church. Two Masses every Sunday during the school year. Because I didn't want to learn Latin Mass responses as an altar boy, I was picked for the choir. Ironic that I had four years of Latin at the Prep! The altar boys even got a day off occasionally by assisting at a funeral Mass during school time, and the two servers usually received a few dollars when helping at a Saturday wedding ceremony. What did a choir boy receive for singing at another Mass yearly at Christmas at the veterans' hospital? We received a large Hersey bar when we returned to Our Lady of Mercy's school auditorium. Big deal! And the boys' choir performed for the congregation at the annual St. Patrick's Day Irish Night. The girls of OLM entertained by singing and dancing also, but the boys were (probably) the headliners.

During the school year, we were taught to go to Confession on Saturdays to get forgiveness for our sins, mortal and venial. I remember one of our Dominican nuns telling us that "one thousand venial sins don't equal one mortal sin!" Want to know the difference? Get a Baltimore Catechism, and read. Perhaps this was the genesis of "Catholic guilt" fostered upon us by the Catholic Church. None of my friends ever went to "confess" to any priest other than Monsignor O'L. No matter what you did, your "penance" was three "Our Father" and two to three "Hail Mary." You were now "good" to receive Holy Communion on Sunday.

As for Monsignor, he was a driving force in Bronx politics, mainly because most of the Democratic voters were Irish and Italian during my elementary and high school years. Example: during the '30s and '40s, the Windsor Theatre on Kingsbridge Road was famous for vaudeville, former Broadway shows with original cast members, and terrific movies: "A" and "B" pictures, cowboy movies, cartoons, and a Flash Gordon serial. The Windsor, unfortunately, showed a C-rated Catholic Legion of Decency movie (*The Moon Is Blue*) one time, and O'L used his influence to get the theater closed in the early 1950s. I do remember Mae West leaving the former movie house via the rear (on Bainbridge Avenue) fire escapes with two muscle men accompanying her. I was about twelve to thirteen years old and asked Chuck D who she was. CD knew everything, to my way of thinking. CD went to Fordham Prep. For the record, I took Emilie to a Mae West movie on our third date in Manhattan to get her response, or lack thereof, of Ms. West. At least Em wasn't too negative about my then favorite movie star.

At least these two latest remembrances above were somewhat serious in nature, notably the confessional comments, but what follows is a pathetic forewarning of what religious power of righteous followers were/are subjected to by the Catholic hierarchy. When I was a little boy and for a few of those years, Our Lady of Mercy published the collections taken at Christmas and Easter in its Sunday bulletins distributed at Sunday Mass. I remember reading at the "$100 contribution level" were two doctors in my neighborhood; spiraling downward to the "$2 contribution" (and probably $1) were some names I recognized. "Mrs. H" donated $2 into the collection basket ably handled pew by pew by the Usher Society men. This was written by name in the Sunday bulletin. Every name was so listed up to the two doctors I mentioned above. This was an outrage. One gave according to one's means, ostensibly, and it was no one's business regarding one's financial contribution to one's church. God knows what you give to your church. He's all that matters! This summoned up the New Testament giving by the poor widow who gave two copper coins at the Temple (Mark 12:41–44). Read it for yourself. To this day, even FP mails to all alumni what everyone gives at its annual written fundraiser, by name. Catholic guilt in action.

A Few Other "Highlights" from OLM and the Class of 1956

In seventh grade, I was captain of the Patrol Boys and picked some of my friends as "lieutenants." One was my lifelong friend, Johnny D'A. Very smart in school, Johnny became a superstar in corporate law after college and law school. Growing up together, I saw his ferocious competitive nature. Charlie C and George E were also named lieutenants. Our job, er, their job, was to see that the boys left the classrooms in an orderly fashion, and those going home for lunch left directly without standing around. Being careful crossing the streets was also our responsibility. We didn't get any "reward" for these duties, but it probably helped build a responsible character trait in us, I guess. Same system at school day's end. My friends were very efficient.

The boys had dance lessons taught by Ms. Shields on a monthly basis. Bryan McG and I were partners doing the Charleston, Mexican Hat Dance, and skip marching. Boy, I'm old! Bryan loves to tell this "fable" why he became a cop. As dancing partners, sans girls, Bryan wants everyone to know that dancing with a guy wasn't manly for him. Hence, he became a cop. Yeah, I'm tired of it also. The funny part of our dance lessons was the skipping part. One of our classmates just couldn't skip. Just couldn't. As "luck" would have it, this eighth grade classmate of mine came to class one day and was about fifteen minutes late. Sister G warned this student, a very good student, by the way, and a Fordham Prep graduate-to-be, not to be late to class tomorrow. He was late again the next day. As if a sudden streak of lightning just appeared, this elderly nun dashed across the room toward the entrance door and booted Philip W in the rear so hard that Philip skipped into the coatroom. Ms. Shields would have been proud.

Another Bryan McG story seems appropriate. The fad at one time was "chestnut" fights. A chestnut was fastened on a shoestring, and one's chestnut struck your opponent's chestnut. The loser's total victories were zeroed out and added to the victor's overall total. For some strange reason, McG's old cruddy chestnut usually won. His lousy chestnut was almost one hundred bouts old! Only later did we find out that Bryan had some clear hardening polishing liquid on his chestnut. Cheat and don't get caught. And my dancing partner became a very good and decorated police detective. Who knew?

Another pastime while at OLM was "card flipping," except for that one time with Johnny D'A, when he wiped me out of my flipping cards, not my mint cards. I always won once I learned the "art of scaling" cards from a neighborhood kid we nicknamed "Florida" because his parent's car carried a Florida license plate. He and I scaled cards against a building wall, and the closest to the wall was the winner. Cover the opponent's card, you won. Scale a "leaner" against the sidewalk and building's edge and you also won, unless your opponent knocked your scaled card down. I wasn't doing too well when I eagerly watched how "Florida" scaled his cards. He held a card between his thumb and his index finger and "wristed" the card. It automatically skids along the ground to the building's edge just about every time. I practiced and practiced until I was invincible. After my reputation preceded me in OLM's boys' schoolyard, I needed cohorts to enter a contest for me. Duke and Bryan were my "associates" in this scheme. I supplied the cards and took 10 percent of their (hopefully) winnings: my choice of the litter. Should either be on a losing streak, I was summoned to enter the contest. Very successful business, indeed.

In fifth grade Confirmation class, Sister P was our instructor. We were ten years old. The strict discipline for understanding the seriousness of becoming "soldiers of Christ" by the receiving of this sacrament of Confirmation administered by a bishop was daily impressed upon us by this wonderful nun. Please note that Confirmation can only be performed by a bishop in the Catholic Church in my "era." The Episcopal Church also only allowed a bishop to bestow this church sacrament. Other faiths allowed a priest or minister to confirm a boy or girl. Michael D found out one day about strict attention when he was found chewing gum in class. This was a no-no anytime in Sister P's classroom. Mike D was banished from the Confirmation class that day. He was allowed back the next day and followed the rules thereafter.

Last but not least was Christmas versus Easter in fifth grade with Sister N, my favorite. Sister N asked the class, "What is the most important day in the Catholic Church?"

I raised my hand and blurted out, "Christmas!"

"Wrong, L," Sister N replied. "It's Easter. Christ rose from the dead on our Easter."

I retorted that Christ had to be born before he could die. Sister N told me and the class that God didn't have to be born. He could have just showed up, my words, not Sister N's words. I couldn't understand that until I got to high school. Something about a theology lesson. The Jesuits were smart teachers.

Falling in Love at Thirteen . . . with Art Museums

Our Lady of Mercy started my love affair with (almost) any type of museum. After all, New York City has "tons" of museums with which to enjoy. New York will always be the "capital of the world." Sorry, Paris! It all started in 1955, when I was in eighth grade with Ms. Cranford, our school art teacher. Now you must remember that competitive scholarship was paramount with several of my classmates: Eddie C, Duke D, Johnny D'A, and Phil W, among others. Eddie and Philip could really draw, and "art" was one of the components of getting the highest report card average. I was awful drawing items, but fortunately, Eddie and Johnny were in the other eighth grade class. To get extra credit in the art report card component, Ms. Cranford gave us several small pictures to research at the Metropolitan Museum of Art and one picture hanging in the New York Historical Society. This latter treasure trove is still relatively unknown to most New Yorkers, but what a place! The famous painting of the Pilgrims and Indians crossing in the snow on "Thanksgiving" was housed at this museum. The Museum of Natural History is exquisite as is the Museum of the City of New York. And I cannot forget the Frick Collection on 5th Avenue and 70th Street. I am not enamored with the Museum of Modern Art; most times I didn't know what I was viewing.

When I was employed by Pan Am, Em and I visited the Louvre several times for the greatest of all portraits: *Mona Lisa*. I also visited the Rijksmuseum in Amsterdam and the Museo del Prado in Madrid, among others. We took our boys to many of the finest museums in Manhattan so that they would appreciate in person the wonders of the art world. Of course, the boys were shown the dinosaurs on many occasions.

OLM Graduation: No Sister and Fordham Prep Baseball and My Father Missing the Bus to Fordham University

A little history: In kindergarten, all children received a Salk polio vaccine. If I remember correctly, only one mother was called to take her "little darling" home. He was crying too much and disturbing the classroom. Yup! It was I. My mother came in ten minutes. We lived on Marion Avenue just north of Fordham Road, and Our Lady of Mercy school was on Marion Avenue, just south of Fordham Road.

In first grade, my dear mother met occasionally at Forbes Restaurant, really a classy diner, with some of the other women who had boys at OLM. (Boys and girls were segregated from each other beginning with the first grade.) One of the ladies was bragging about her son as mothers might do from time to time. This, apparently, was incessant with this particular mother. My mother said nothing because I didn't talk about school often when I was home. Dad was a fireman and always working or so it seemed. My two brothers were younger than I and not in elementary school as yet. In fact, in kindergarten, when my mother went for a teacher-parent discussion about little LD, mom was taken aback by the Maryknoll nun's comment: "Not to worry about your son. He's, by far, the smartest in the class, both the boys and girls. He's just a little too quiet and shy." This wasn't the only surprise for my dear mother.

We had two classrooms for the eighth grade boys. I can only suggest happenings in the other eighth grade class, except that my lifelong friends, Eddie C and Johnny D'A, took the entrance test and were granted scholarships to Regis High School in Manhattan, to this day the best Catholic high school in the country and scholarship-only acceptance. *Dr. Anthony Fauci is a graduate of Regis High School. Yes, that AF of COVID-19 fame.*

Sister G called me into the back of our classroom and offered me the opportunity to take the entrance exam for Regis High School. I demurred, saying I didn't want to go to Regis. I wanted to attend Fordham Preparatory School. I didn't mention that Regis didn't have a baseball team, and I wanted to be a professional baseball player when I was older. Sister would have "killed" me had I mentioned my reasoning. My father was called in for a chat with Sister G to convince my father that I should take the exam for Regis. It was a terrific honor just to take the exam. My father said to Sister G, "Why deprive another boy from taking the test for Regis when my son, Louie, will not attend Regis even should he win a scholarship? Louie's going to Fordham Prep."

Simple logic since only three boys from each eighth grade class were eligible to sit for the examination. In my class, only KD got a scholarship to Regis. The other two boys in my classroom failed the test. Oh! My father was scheduled to take the entrance exam for Fordham Prep himself, got on a bus to Fordham University, and asked the bus driver to alert my father when the bus got within walking distance of the Fordham campus. The driver forgot, and my father arrived at City Island in the Bronx much too far to walk to the Prep. My dad missed the test and had to "settle" for Stuyvesant High School in Manhattan, to this day, still one of the best public high schools in NYC.

Let's fill in the blanks regarding eighth grade graduation and that reference to Forbes Restaurant above. The boys sat on the left side facing the altar, and the girls sat on the right facing the altar. After many awards to the boys' graduating class, with recognition to Ken "Duke" D, Eddie C, and Johnny D'A, the boy with highest regents examinations average would be awarded a gold watch: a Bulova Senator wristwatch with an inscription on the back: OLM Ushers 1956. (No idea about the girls' awards!) The watch was awarded to LD, and I proceeded to the altar's front steps to receive the watch from OLM's pastor with about six other priests standing behind the pastor. Monsignor asked me why I didn't take the test for Regis High School. In a loud voice, not really, but it seemed so at the time, I remarked quite nervously, "I didn't want to go there, Sister!"

Good God! What an embarrassment! Some of the guys heard my response, and I saw a few roll their eyes. God only knows what the girls who might have heard me thought. What a jerk! Topped only by graduation from Fordham Prep four years later!

So here's what happened at the 1960 Fordham Prep graduation in Fordham University's gymnasium. My father and mother were present. Brothers MB and JJ were there also, along with several of my relatives. The gym was packed for the 199 graduating seniors out of 250 starting in 1956. Every boy (all-boys high school) wore a white dinner jacket with the accompanying black striped pants. The recipient of the diploma walked up three steps on the left, took the diploma from Father Shea (I think!), turned around and bowed, descended the three steps on the right, and proceeded to his seat. Simple. Nothing to it. This was done in alphabetical order. Well, "yours truly" walked up the three steps, took the diploma and bowed to the audience, and proceeded down the three steps to my seat. Not exactly. All went well until I left the stage and started down the three steps to return to my seat. I tripped and fell down the three steps, and when I arose from the gym floor, there were many footprints on the white jacket that my mother rented for this "solemn" occasion. What a clumsy so-and-so.

The family went to Jahn's Ice Cream Parlor on Kingsbridge Road to celebrate LD's high school graduation. My father made me wear that jacket throughout the evening. I have no idea what happened when my dear mother returned the jacket and pants. I never asked. I filed this experience for a future reminder to watch what I'm doing.

Missing First Day of High School Together with Going to School with My Freshman Pal JJO'RIII Footnote: Father Edward P, SJ

Eighth grade was now just a memory. In September 1956, I was starting Fordham Prep, the same Jesuit high school where my dear friend CD would be a senior. Looking forward to the first day of class at the Prep . . . I missed the first day of class at the Prep. My father knew someone, who knew someone, and I spent my first day of class at a tryout for the New York Yankees. At thirteen years of age, when the minimum age was sixteen! Very humiliating, but the scouts at the Stadium were kind. No snickering and no "Let's go, kid. Next."

My dad knew of my desire to become a professional baseball player, but after I got older, more experienced, and could handle a defeat without any excuses. Anyone could handle winning graciously.

Whenever you missed school, you provided a note to the teacher. At the Prep, this "teacher" was the Prefect of Discipline, the above named Rev. Arthur V. Shea, SJ. Picture his expression when I handed Father S a note: "Please excuse my son, Louie, for missing school yesterday. He was at Yankee Stadium, trying out to become a professional baseball player. Signed, Mary D."

Father said nothing about the note, just "Have a good day. Now get to class."

I was now on his "watch list." Not good, my friends. Not good!

All went well that second day and in the days to come. I loved Fordham Prep. I still do to this day.

About the same time every day, eight o'clock in the morning, I walked from my apartment house east toward Fordham University, passing the New York Central Railroad, Fordham Road station. After several days, I recognized one of my homeroom guys walking in the same direction as me. I introduced myself as did he: John O'R, soon to be known as John J O'RIII in algebra class. I was given the moniker LDIII and Eddie M was EMIII. Mr. Edward P (in a few more years to become Father EP) gave us those names. Funny man!

Since I've gone off on a tangent and mentioned our algebra teacher, here's how "funny" Mr. P was. Over the Easter vacation, Mr. P assigned us algebra homework, the only teacher so inclined. Many of us were upset; one unhappy enough to write a note when submitting the homework by postal service: me. I wrote and told Mr. P that homework was unfair to us "holiday lovers." Am I crazy or what? Mr. P had the "board of education" and utilized it on your rear, should you talk during his class instruction. I shuddered to think what he'd do to that letter writer. I discarded the note and posted my algebra homework. School was back in session, and we had algebra immediately after lunch. At lunch, one of my OLM friends, Richie K, related how some "nut job" sent a nasty note to Mr. P about giving us homework over Easter. I said nothing. I threw the damn note away. Lunch over, we returned to the classroom, and when Mr. P entered, he looked in my direction. "Before we begin," Mr. P stated, "I'd like to read you what one of your fellow students wrote to me."

Good God! I mailed the comment I had "thought." I'm dead! The guys were breathing quite heavily when Mr. P asked me what I thought of this affront to a Jesuit teacher. I responded, "Mister, the person who sent that to you knew you had a great sense of humor and would get a chuckle or two."

"Mr. LD, I'll see you in my office after school . . . today."

I'm dead. I'll be thrown out of the Prep. My father would kill me.

I met Mr. P in his office, and he put a spotlight lamp directly on me and gave me a sex talk. Mr. P desired to be a Student Counselor when finally ordained, and he "practiced" on me. That was it, neither "board of education" nor expulsion from school.

Footnote: Father Edward P. returned to Fordham Prep as its Student Counselor. We became good friends after that Easter note. We even went to dinner at the Lido Riviera Restaurant (Kingsbridge Road off Fordham Road, two blocks from my home and about ten minutes' walk from Fordham's campus and Jesuit housing) when Father P started the fall school semester in 1960. While I offered to pay for dinner, Father paid. I inquired, "Why? I thought Jesuits took the vow of poverty, along with chastity and obedience."

Father P replied, "We always have petty cash available . . . just in case!"

As a footnote, I was invited to EP's inauguration after his final vows but didn't attend the Maryland ceremony. In hindsight, I should have gone to see my friend consecrated as a Jesuit priest. I told Brother JJ, another Prep graduate, if he should have any difficulty in school, see Father P for advice. Sadly, at the end of JJ's first semester, Father died of neck cancer.

That said and moving forward, every school day thereafter, I waited for JO'R to exit the Fordham Road station, and we walked together to the Prep. JO'R lived in Scarsdale and played "touch" football and softball as I did. We also chatted about the homework from the previous night and together with five other 1F freshmen, sat outside the Prep building, "comparing" the homework assignments from yesterday. The other guys, if I can remember, were John LaC, Henry H, Billy C, Tom C, and Jimmy C. One time (at least) some of the guys copied my homework. Freshmen were on the fourth floor. (Each succeeding year, one went one floor down toward the main senior floor.) This one time, as maybe two guys were copying my Latin homework, a bird in the tree above us crapped on my homework. The bell rang and everyone ran to the stairs and didn't want to be late for catechism class. Everyone but "yours truly." I had to clean the damn notebook paper. I just made my classroom seat before the opening bell rang. When I handed in my Latin assignment, our Latin teacher, Mr. Jack S. just looked at the paper and then to me. I wouldn't let that happen again, and no more sitting on a bench under that tree.

JO'R and I usually met at the train station to compare class notes. And we did play "touch" football and softball together. In fact, we lost to the sophomores for the lower division "touch" championship but beat their "butts" to become the lower division softball champions. We each received a small plastic trophy, which was my first award in any sporting events. I had that precious reminder with me for sixty years until I moved from one location in Ohio to another. The only trophy I still have in my possession is the "Intramural Athlete of the Year" from Fordham University, received when I was a senior at the university. I did keep all those memories with me wherever I relocated, especially that trophy win with my 1F teammates. Sadly, only two of those guys were with me in the science honors class for the following three years. The others were either in the classical honors or regular academic programs. JJO'RIII was not in my honors class, but we did go to Fordham University and its School of Business, along with about twenty other Prep graduates. Most college men went to local schools in the late '50s and early '60s.

Jack J. O'RIII and Intramural Football—
Prep and the University

One last—actually, two remembrances with my friend JJO'RIII, if I may. My science honors class (4F) with Frank L, Henry H, and Billy C from our 1F crew played Jack O'R's academic class (4A) for the upper division championship, "touch" football, in senior year at the Prep. We started with a handicap: Frank, Henry, Billy, and several others weren't on Edwards Parade to start the game. Something happened in the locker room that delayed their attendance. What to do? I could quarterback, but who would catch the ball? We decided—I decided that Jim M, our scholar, would quarterback. Well, no finger-pointing at Jim, but when Frank et al. arrived, we were down 20-0. The playing field was slippery because of the wet grass, and Frank did slip several times. We left the grounds and discussed the fact that we were not at full strength because of the locker room fiasco with the Athletic Director, Father Thomas G, SJ, who just happened to be JJO'RIII's homeroom teacher! In only a Jesuit's logic, Father Thomas G determined that we would start the second half down 20-0. Have you ever played "touch" and tried to score three TDs in one half? Nearly impossible! Jack's class got zero, and we scored three times, but only one extra point, losing 20-19. On the last TD, I was open in the end zone, but Frank overthrew me. We needed that extra point. We were robbed. In college, and as luck would have it, in senior year at the "B" School, my section team played Jack's section's team. We won 6-0 when I intercepted Jack's pass and ran it in for the winning score. Vindicated! Finally and on our way to becoming university champs!

At out fiftieth Prep reunion in 2010, after Jack and I hugged each other, JJO'RIII reminded LDIII that his class beat us in "touch" fifty years ago for the Prep championship. That damn O'R will never let me forget it! I love him anyway.

More Father Shea, SJ: Love Him or Hate Him

Okay, the nuns were gone, and Fordham Prep was finally here. Let me tell you about the Jesuit priest we disliked as a freshman but loved after graduation: the legendary AVS, SJ. You can surmise my feelings— and many, many others'—for this man of God by several examples. You then decide if I'm being truthful. I came to school one day wearing a crew-neck sweater over my tie. That's the way one wore this type of sweater! Father S was standing by the front door, watching for the students to arrive. "Artie" saw me, and his eye contact "called" me to him. "Son, go visit the mirror in the locker room," was Father's comment. Downstairs, I hurried and in front of the floor-to-ceiling mirror, made sure my tie was showing over my sweater. "Very good, son. Have a good day." What a lot of crap, I thought. As a freshman and possibly a sophomore, to get your attention, Father would hold up one or two fingers. Oh! Oh! Artie wants to see us. You hustled to him, and he asked what you were doing. Your "Catholic guilt" made you tell him. Usually, you were only chastised and went on your way. As you got older—and wiser—one realized that Father AVS, SJ held up two fingers to trap you. He couldn't possibly see everything that everyone was doing. When you were fooling around, when you shouldn't, and the two fingers went into the air, you ignored them and continued whatever you were doing. No dire consequence by ignoring Father. He never saw what you did.

Another time LD was sitting in Webster Park with several of the guys after a Prep home basketball game. (Webster Park was on the other side of the Fordham campus, separated only by the NY Central Railroad.) One or two of my classmates were smoking—not allowed anywhere but the Senior Room in the Prep basement—and we were not seniors yet! Someone yelled, "There's Artie!"

We all scattered. We escaped. I knew the lay of the land and "disappeared" but still panicked. For the rest of our tenure at the Prep, no one who was there that night ever mentioned our narrow escape. This was the fear that Father S instilled in us, "Always comport yourself with dignity. If you know something is wrong, own up to it and accept the consequence when confronted. You'll more quickly become the man we're training you to become." That was Father Shea. Two years removed from the Prep and being with some of my classmates at the annual Prep reunion, AVS rose to address the alumni. He softly stated,

"I'll tell you what's wrong with America today. They don't make the Prep man like they used to." Father was, shall we say, in conflict with the current administration at the Prep when he said this. Every member of every class that graduated from Fordham Prep with "Artie" as Prefect of Discipline stood and applauded for two to three minutes. Some cheered. The current "powers that be" in the Prep could be seen fuming. That was AVS, SJ.

One last situation, if I may, in 1972, Brother JJ got married in the Fordham University Chapel. On the receiving line, I glanced out the main entrance and saw Father Shea. I whispered to Brother JJ, "There's Artie outside."

We left JJ's wife greeting people she hardly knew because we went outside to talk with Father Shea. I personally hadn't seen him in twelve years. I made sure my bow tie was straightened as did my youngest brother! We loved that Jesuit priest.

My Friend Jerry P and the Start of My Really Playing Baseball

Wanting to be a major league baseball player in the future, I couldn't spend my time playing stickball, corner ball, and other mundane athletics with my neighborhood Decatur Avenue (Bronx) friends any longer. Besides, they now became interested in girls. My time with women would have to wait until later. (As a freshman at the Prep, I won two tickets to any Broadway show in a school fundraiser. Not having a girlfriend, I gave the tickets to my mother, who went to see *My Fair Lady* with her sister, my Godmother, Aunt Betty. Mom also received $20 from the Prep in this winning raffle package. Not bad for a $2 entry fee!)

I wandered to various ball fields and schoolyards in the Bronx, looking for a game of BB or softball. Pick-up games were nice practice, but I was a pitcher and center fielder, and being a lefty, I was limited to the positions I could play in this very difficult sport. Fact: Throw ten passes in football and complete three, you're not very good; take ten shots in a basketball game and make three, you're not very good; in baseball, come to bat ten times and get three hits, you're an All-Star. I was an All-Star.

One day I was talking with Jerry P, and he suggested that I play with his sandlot team, the Blue Jays. He would chat with the team's manager and see if I could get on its roster. Not only on the roster, but I also started the game at Frankie Frisch Field, a legendary baseball field to all Bronx kids. The prior starting pitcher, Ronnie I, wasn't too happy, but he got over it. He and I became good friends, played hoops at the playground on Webster Avenue and East 188th Street with Jerry and played softball together for many years. Playing for the Blue Jays and organized baseball for the first time, I would always owe the start of "true" baseball for me to my dearest friend, Jerry P.

After the 1958 summer baseball season, I was the MVP of our PAL League while I played for the Blue Jays. At the awards celebration, the guest speaker was George "Snuffy" Stirnweiss (Fordham Prep grad and former second baseman for the New York Yankees). He and I chatted about FP and baseball. What a gentleman who took the time to talk with this sixteen-year-old kid. Tragically, Mr. Stirnweiss died in a New Jersey passenger train wreck September 15, 1958. Many years later, 2001 to be exact, I was sitting in the Fordham University chapel for a Memorial Mass for those Prepsters who lost their lives on September 11. Next to me was Snuffy's brother, Andrew, Prep Class of 1941. He related that had his brother not have been such an athlete (stolen base champ in the American League while with the NYY), he, running to catch the train leaving the station platform, would not have made the train and would still have had many more years on this earth. True story, so help me, God! Shortly thereafter, I had another tryout at Yankee Stadium, this time aware of probing eyes watching my every move on the pitcher's mound. This one "hot shot" just out of college and signed for zillions by the Yankees was hitting all my batting practice throws into the right field stands. I asked the scout behind me if I might "try to get this guy out." Denied and told to continue with putting the ball over the plate for this lefty hitter, I told myself, BS! I curved him, his knees buckled, and I was removed from the pitcher's mound. For the history, this "turkey" never played major league BB. One has to hit more than just a fast ball. Every major leaguer can hit a fastball . . . most of the time.

Back to Jerry. Jerry was on the Regis High School basketball team, and while JP was really only interested in basketball, he wasn't that bad as a catcher in "my" sport. I'll never forget that Jerry P took the time, with no personal reward, to get me started "on my way" to playing high school and college baseball and the opportunity to sign with a major league baseball team after my college days. The latter I declined for several personal reasons.

JP and I sat for a doughnut and coffee/tea at a Twin Donut store after one of the Blue Jays game. Ha! A thought came to my mind. We always used Mike D's leaded bat before our turn at that bat. At the plate, it "made" our bat lighter and, hence, quicker bat speed. "Bat speed" dictated how far a baseball would travel, not body strength, unlike slo-pitch softball, where the opposite is true. I told Jerry that we should develop a metal "doughnut" to carry with our baseball bag and make use of the doughnut when we came to bat. A few swings and tap the bat on the plate to remove the metal donut. No longer did we need a leaded bat. Besides, Mike's leaded bat wasn't always available. Brilliant! Unfortunately, I didn't do it. Note: As it turned out, Elston Howard of the NYY/Boston Red Sox "invented" this apparatus. This metal doughnut is now universally utilized in baseball primarily and in fast-pitch softball.

Going on Family Vacation in New York State and Returning Home Alone

One summer, when I was almost seventeen, my parents took us on a vacation to Upstate New York. My father was always working, especially during his tenure as a fireman, and we rarely left the Bronx. This particular summer my father thought, with a trip upstate, we might enjoy the history of New York before and after the Revolutionary War. We went to Fort Ticonderoga, Lake Champlain, and points there around. Very interesting, but I had a few baseball games I was missing. I asked my father if I might take a train home. Knowing my love and desire for baseball, my dad put me on an NY Central train destined for NYC. Somehow I got to the Fordham Road station, and knowing where I was, I walked to our apartment for the night. Tomorrow: baseball game. Because this was my first night ever alone in the apartment, I put a chair against our locked front door of the apartment and slept with a knife under my pillow. What a brave guy! I got very little sleep. I think I jabbed myself once with the butter knife. Every noise I heard kept me awake. By the way, it rained, and we didn't play. My brothers had a terrific time, but my mother was upset with me. Apparently, Brother MB requested to get a train to the Bronx the next day. My father just looked at MB and was never asked again to go home and stay with Brother L. Brother JJ knew better than to say he wanted to return home also. Another future Fordham Prep graduate and Boston College grad! Many years later I traveled upstate with Emilie and our two sons. Had a great time!

The Bronx and Pine Bush, New York House

It took several years of hard work by my father, but with the grace of God, dad's house was finished (with Uncle John F providing the plumbing work), and in 1959, we had a definite summer vacation spot in the "country" and the Shawangunk Mountains in Orange County, New York State (about two hours from our apartment building in the Bronx). Only my mother and I didn't enjoy being there because we were "city folks." My father and two younger brothers truly relished the trip. Brother MB actually stayed there while at Marist College in Poughkeepsie, New York.

This one visit the "local" bees were quite disturbing, to say the least. Alongside the south side of the house was a bare-branched tree about sixty feet in the air with this humungous beehive, with constantly swirling bees. LD had an idea: As everyone got into the family car, LD stood outside—with the back passenger door wide open for my escape upon the success of my plan—and hurled a large-enough stone at the beehive. Bull's eye on the first attempt! The hive came plummeting to the ground and smashed apart like a cook breaking eggs to make an omelet. I dove into the car, and off dad drove down the gravel road like he was propelling his hook and ladder fire apparatus in an emergency. My father related that there were no "busy bees" upon his next visit to Pine Bush, sans mom and eldest son, naturally.

I mention this incident for when you get to the part where I "won" a stuffed animal for Emilie (my future wife but girlfriend at the time) when we visited the Danbury, Connecticut fair. Stay tuned.

"Touch" Football with the Boys at Fordham—"Big" GT and DH Stealing Second and Flipping over Second Base

Not everything was fun and games for me, LD. I hung out with guys on Decatur Avenue (another Bronx street parallel to Webster Avenue and perpendicular to Fordham Road). During football season, we walked to Fordham University and played "touch" with tackling on the grass closest to the NY Central. When campus security was spotted by us, we "disappeared" by finding an opening in the iron-barred fence to escape. We knew the ins and outs of not getting caught where we knew we didn't belong.

This one time we were playing "tackle" football without pads instead of just "two-handed touch." Evading "Big" George T, he pushed Dennis H into my right leg, and something stretched in the knee area. Down I went like a bull elephant hit by a rash of bullets. Game over for me. I limped home and iced my right knee. The next day I could hardly walk. A few days later, I visited Dr Dan M, who had an office in our apartment building. This terrific physician drained my knee of fluid so that I could walk without too much difficulty. The morale of this story: Don't trespass where you don't belong, or be careful you don't get caught after you get injured—something like that.

My right knee bothered me often the rest of my high school ball playing and throughout my college days. I loved the competitive challenges and always played with a brace on my knee. My neighborhood friends knew my "secret," but no one else found out. One time we played against my Blue Jays baseball team— my neighborhood guys wouldn't play baseball against the Blue Jays unless I pitched for them. I looked forward to beating my sandlot team. On first base, I decided to steal second. Their shortstop covered second and faked the ball being thrown from the Blue Jay catcher, Dom B. I looked back for a second and saw that Johnny DV was faking catching a thrown baseball. You don't do that because the sliding base stealer could get injured without a play happening. That's exacted what transpired: I hit the bag wrong and flipped over—my right knee extended incorrectly. Done for the game. Since we were leading, my guys claimed victory; my Blue Jays opposition said nothing. But my knee was so bad I couldn't ride my bike home. One of my friends took my bike to my building, while another guy "drove" me home on his bike. My knee was never the same after that unsportsmanlike play by JDV. In spite of that, I played all the sports I could, except "tackle" football. Got my knee drained four to six times before I quit playing baseball. My centerfield days playing softball were also over. Thank God I could play first base with little difficulty.

Living in Miami, Florida, the Start of Junior Year

When freshman year was nearly over and during final exams, my closest friends and I played "pitching-in" by the handball courts on campus just behind the Fordham University chapel.

For your information, the chimes that were used for Our Lady of Mercy Church were from that Fordham chapel and inspired Edgar Allan Poe's famous poem, "Bells, Bells, Bells," before he moved from Poe (Park) Cottage (Bronx, New York) to Baltimore, Maryland, where this American icon died in 1849.

This was basically a rectangle painted on a handball wall and where strikes were called, like a baseball game, if one swung at the thrown tennis ball and missed or "took the pitch" and the tennis ball landed inside the rectangle or struck the outline itself. As freshmen, our group was made up of growing athletes. In hindsight, only John LaC and I became future baseball players. One of the others played some football; others were good intramural sportsmen. My budding baseball "vision" was almost steamrolled dead when Jimmy C hit the ball over the handball court behind me. "Hit" was being kind to me. I didn't need to turn around—the ball was "gone." How could this happen? Jimmy C wasn't a baseball player. He was just one of the guys. This couldn't be an omen of my baseball future, I hoped. Thank God our final exam in Latin made me forget this anomaly. Sophomore year tore us apart for good. My 1F friends were put into the classical honors program, but I still had Henry H and Billy C in the science honors program. JJO'RIII wasn't with me. Kenny L was in my class also for the next three years, and for the next three years, I spent time with Frankie LoD, JVM, Tony A, and Wes S. Loved all those guys!

"Poor" John LaC, the rumor was true that John was moving to Florida. How awful. He was on the freshman basketball team, and at least ten of us went to each home game rooting, "We want LaC! We want LaC! Put him in the game!" Yes, he was in classical honors, but John was a "1F guy." He'll be missed.

Surprise! Surprise! The LD family was moving to Florida also that summer. I was devastated. I was leaving my Prep friends forever and leaving my neighborhood friends also. This couldn't be. My two younger brothers didn't mind, neither in high school, and didn't have friends like my friends. I fully realized it did happen when I saw the apartment in Miami. My mother and her three boys arrived first; my father would join us in a few months. Dad was going to work at the local horse racing track through the husband's connections of my mother's best friend in Manhattan who moved to Miami Beach about twenty years prior. Combined with my father's disability pension from the NYC Fire Department, our family would be financially fine. Sounded good, except that my walking to high school was finished. (My two brothers walked to their school from our apartment complex in North Miami.) I took two buses to Archbishop Curley High School—all-boys school again—and wouldn't go unless my mother came with me! What a sissy! After two days, my mother told me to get on the bus to school—alone. High school was okay because I gravitated toward two other ball players—football players. I discovered that the baseball team was terrible, so my chance of continuing my budding baseball career was still a positive force. Classroom "stuff" was quite boring. My Latin class was Caesar; I should have been taking Cicero or whatever one took in third year at this high school. My mother was called to visit the principal regarding her son, L. She was told that a mistake was made. I would be placed in third year Latin and several other senior classes because I apparently was quite ahead of the third year students. Mom replied, "Don't bother. We don't belong here. We're going home to New York!"

My miserable existence here in the Sunshine State was coming to an end. Everyone—mom and I—could live "happily ever after."

Before I finish my sojourn to Florida, I want to share three occurrences with you:

1. I took two buses to school. This particular day I was on my way to school via the first bus, and I was sitting where I usually sat in the Bronx: in the back of the bus. Did you ever get a feeling that someone's watching you, but from where? I realized that the bus driver was trying to get my attention. I went to the front, and the bus driver told me I wasn't allowed to see in the back of the bus. "That's where the %$&*#$% sit!"
    I couldn't believe this. I suggested, "I always sit in the back of the bus."
    I was told again I couldn't sit there, and if I didn't move forward, he'd stop the bus and get the police. Had I been going home

instead of to school, I would have dared the bastard to call the police. I sheepishly moved. This was 1958, folks, not 1858!

2. We were in a Woolworth's-like building, having lunch on a Saturday. I was to watch my two younger brothers. "Where's JJ?" I asked MB.

    Fortunately, JJ was in eyesight standing at the water cooler marked "Colored." JJ thought it was colored water. Another travesty.

3. On the way home that day, we started across the main drag. A Black woman was just in front of us. She saw me, stopped, took a few steps backward, and let us cross ahead of her. I stopped and told her we're from NYC and she was to go ahead of us. This older lady just smiled and ambled across the road.

How dreadful this happened in our country, the "land of the free." I was ashamed for what happened in this last episode. I was almost sixteen, and I saw the prejudices some held against other Americans. This was not right. Very sad, my friends.

As a finishing touch, the four of us took an awful and very long bus ride home to NYC. Mom knocked on the apartment door, and my father was probably one week from wrapping things up in NYC and on to Florida. He couldn't believe we were back. There was a somewhat heated "discussion" between my father and mother, and this was the only time in my life living with my parents—twenty-seven years until I left home when Emilie and I got married—that my mom said "no" to my dad.

Dad and I sat down in the living room, and I was told we were going back to Florida. I started to cry real tears, not like the "fake" tears when I got that sex talk from Mr. Ed P when I was in freshman algebra class. My father knew my love for Fordham Prep and agreed with my mother that we would stay here in the Bronx. After making a few calls to a former firemen's chaplain and former Prep principal, I was accepted back into the Prep, along with MB, who had a Fireman's Scholarship to the Prep and started as a freshman. It didn't hurt our acceptability that I was already in the science honors class.

I only missed the first month of Cicero and math class algorithms. To this day, I don't know what the latter is! I do remember that the first class I attended that October 1 was second year German. I asked the German teacher, "Where do I sit?"

Mr. H retorted, "You sit on your ass!"

Welcome back to Fordham Prep, LD. We missed you, and I missed my friends. What a ride and a living experience, our short time in North Miami, Florida!

Baseball at the Prep and Dropping Throw;
JS and LD HRs Dropping Throw Years Later ('70s) Softball
at VA

Playing baseball and its poor relative, softball, didn't always bring the best out of me. In junior year, while playing first base, I covered first waiting for a throw from our pitcher, Rich N. This right-hander was a very good fielder and upon turning toward me, underhanded a soft toss to me. I took my eye off the ball and closed my first baseman's mitt with the baseball hitting my mitt's closed webbing. Error—first base! Instead of getting upset, our Prep senior just glared at me for a nanosecond and proceeded to strike out the next batter. No harm done, except to me. This would never happen again, I thought.

The following year the Prep played Tolentine High School (Bronx, New York). We looked forward to facing Steve R, he of well-deserved high school baseball fame. Playing first again, I rotated between first base, the pitcher's mound, and left field, our sun field. The latter only when Charlie V wasn't available. We scored the most runs in Fordham Prep history—over thirty runs—but who's counting? No Steve R, though. Tolentine was saving him for a CHSAA play-off game. (The Prep was an independent club during my tenure, so we played mainly public school teams.) John S usually batted fifth in the lineup, and I batted sixth. JS got up one inning and hit an HR over the right field wall into the tennis court. I followed with another drive into the tennis court. The route of Tolentine continued. Next go-around, the opposition had some "stiff" pitching. He hit JS, and I laughed as he trotted to first base. This guy also hit me. JS was laughing at me as he went to second base: two batters, two HBP. I mention this because I want you to know I earned every start as a junior and senior on the Prep's baseball club. God works in mysterious ways: In my senior yearbook, my individual picture was missing. When the photographer was taking snapshots of the pitching staff, I was at first base with fielding practice. When the starting infielders were "posing" for a picture, I was on the sidelines throwing to a catcher. Hence, no picture of me in the yearbook. It happens. Yeah, right!

Moving ahead four years, almost the same happened to befall me when I was a senior at Fordham University. The campus editor of the *Maroon Quill*, the School of Business yearbook (in my time each school published its own yearbook), Richie M, a fellow accounting major, asked me to be the copy editor. He asked several times, and I demurred several times. Finally, I said, "Fine. I'll do it."

Again, God was on my side. Rummaging through the already-prepared pages of the annual, I checked the sports section. Great coverage of the university's sports, even baseball, except where's my individual picture? There was a team picture, our coach, team captain Billy M, Gerry M, and some action photos, but no Steve R, Steve P, and LD! I wouldn't be denied again. Not on my watch. I used my father's Polaroid camera to take pictures of SR and SP for our yearbook; all three of us attended the School of Business, so there would be no problem inserting these two pictures into the baseball section. Hey! One of you has to take my picture! That done, all three were included in the yearbook with ample "applause" in the captions for each of us. As the book's campus copy editor, I "glorified" all three of us for posterity, well, those two anyway! While our close friend SP has passed, I talk often with sports management "superstar" SR. As a postscript, I finished baseball in the Queens Alliance that summer with Grandview Dairy and our college catcher "Dutch" S. I had success as the *Long Island Press* box scores/writeups attested. Perhaps I should have . . .

What about that déjà vu moment, you ask? Many years later, married and playing softball for money, we had an exhibition game at the veterans' hospital in the Bronx, for fun, to "entertain" the hospital patients. I knew someone who knew someone. That's how we got to the hospital's barely-adequate ball field. Late in the game, as we were steamrolling the opponents, their batter hit a slow roller to me at first base. While a five-year-old would have picked up the softball with his small fingers, I allowed the ball to pass under my legs for an error. As I retrieved the softball, one of the patients watching the game from the small grandstands yelled out, "Hey, first base! Why don't you put your glove (*mitt* is the proper terminology) away and sell peanuts in the stands?"

Everyone heard him. I gave a quick look and saw that the "commentator" was a veteran seated in a wheelchair. For several months thereafter, when we were in our home sponsor's bar, a few of my fellow teammates asked the bartender if he had any peanuts for the bar. I deserved the ribbing.

THE 1960S

Basically Fordham University (FU)
Coupled with Corporate Employment
Last of the Prep and James V M: Teaching the Teacher
Tony C, Second Best

How would you like to be a bridesmaid but never a bride? Rhetorically speaking, that is! In case you were not aware, men aren't bridesmaids!

James V M was no. 1 on the "smarts" list graduating from Fordham Prep. This future Notre Dame graduate and future PhD in nuclear physics from Yale University was no nerd. Jim was president of our class section for our three years together. Down-to-earth JVM never lauded over anyone because of his God-given abilities. He never—that I saw—took a textbook home to study. While I'm sure he had to do so—this was Fordham Prep—his recitals in senior year Latin and English were superb. Jim listened to others give their answers or recitals in class and repeated everything word for word. He answered all the questions put to him and never raised his hand to self-boost that he knew the answer. The only time I truly think he was stumped in Latin was the time Fr. John Leonard, SJ played a synonym name with us. Father L gave a Latin word, and we had to come up with a synonym. This one time Father L gave us the word "imperium" and asked for a synonym in Latin. Jim was probably bored and didn't respond. No one else did either. I raised my hand, was recognized by Father L quite quizzically, and gave my riposte, "res, rei. F." RES means "thing" in law and could stand for most anything. Brilliant, I thought, but taking my life into my hands by making a mockery of this Latin game of Father L was quite foolish.

Father L didn't like to be upstaged, especially that one time a Jesuit visitor sat in the back of the room while Father L, SJ was giving us a solid geometry lesson. JVM corrected Father L not once, but twice. Father L asked our visitor to join him outside the room. Father L stormed out! We all knew we were in big trouble when he returned—alone. We were given twenty-five lines of "The Aeneid" to translate for tomorrow's Latin class instead of the usual fifteen lines. Thanks, JVM!

We had SATs for one of the prerequisites for college acceptance. Mr. JVM got 800 in English and in math. Out of a possible 800. He also got 792 in advanced placement chemistry and wanted to know what he got wrong. Yet "Vinny" played intramural football with us and was in every school organization one could imagine. After his name and picture in our 1960 yearbook, this "Person from Another World" had ten lines of extracurricular after his name. The average was no more than three. Remarkable!

As for the no. 2 scholar in our graduating class, Tony C, he too was in my science honors program. How would you like to have a cumulative four-year average of 96+ and finish second to the JVM "machine"? A very quiet guy in class, TC never was jealous of JVM, or so it seemed. Another brilliant scholar, TC also was an athlete as a member of the school's track team. We didn't "hang out" together because the track guys, regardless of being in an honors program or not, were a close-knit group who worked out together and just concentrated on their sport. AC was admired by all his classmates, and I'm 100 percent positive that Tony became "no. 1" in any venture in which he participated in his future life. God bless James and Tony, my Fordham Prep classmates and friends.

1962 Home Runs at Frisch Field and Macombs Dam Park
The Blonde, Bike Ride, and the Bazaar in '62

In '60 and '61, I played baseball with some special teammates. Playing with St. Mary's RC Church on White Plains Road was quite an experience. I pitched along with Paul G (a Manhattan College future graduate and Bronx DA) and the best baseballer I ever played with or against: Carl L, a superb outfielder, magnificent RBI man, our clutch go-to guy, and the leader of our team. We usually split a Saturday doubleheader, and the following doesn't reflect my playing with the St. Mary's Buccaneers but brings me to the game in which I participated and won in the bottom of the ninth inning with two outs. In an "invitation only" baseball game, John M was our star catcher, who played behind Charlie Silvera and the immortal Yogi Berra of the Bronx Bombers themselves. I pitched a complete game, and the manager—sorry, I don't remember his name— kept me in this tie game probably more than he should have, considering I threw more than one hundred pitches. But I am grateful he did. In the bottom of the ninth with two outs, as mentioned, I was allowed to hit. Don't remember the count, but I hit a deep high fly over the right field fence, over the highway exit ramp, and into a Yankees home game parking lot. Game over. Because JM had high minor league experience, I asked him if I should stay as a pitcher or should I become a "position player" because I could hit. "Stick to pitching" was JM's retort. So I did.

In late summer of 1962, Our Lady of Mercy (my Bronx church) played Transfiguration Church of Manhattan at venerable Frankie Frisch Field off Webster Avenue and near the RR tracks of the NY Central (now the Metro) Botanical Garden station. In the bottom of the first inning, with my good friend Danny K on first, I hit another deep high fly over the "almost" dead center field fence, over the El train tracks, hitting the sixth floor of the apartment building across the street. Game over. The final score was a 7-0 shutout with everyone hitting: "Big" George T, Richie B, and our terrific catcher for most of the season, Bobby A—an All-City football player, who happened to be a member of the younger Blue Jays Baseball Club when I played with the older Blue Jays in Bronx sandlot summer baseball. Three other former Blue Jays also were on our winning team: Jerry G, Ronnie I, and John O'S. Can't leave them out. Our coach, Mr. John Brown, showed me the rudiments of playing first base—he who played minor league Triple A baseball behind Gail Harris and Whitey Lockman of the NY and SF Giants. Mr. Brown showed me some "tricks" at first that I used successfully during my time playing in various softball leagues as I got older and ceased playing baseball. Oh! JB played in the Giants system with Willie Mays and Monte Irvin—both Hall of Famers in Cooperstown at Minneapolis. I had a great instructor in Mr. B.

Now, in the winter of 1962, some of my Decatur Avenue friends and I stopped by OLM while a fundraising bazaar was in session. I also met some of my OLM grad friends there. Dave C's father was at the "wheel of fortune" and saw us. He used the stage microphone to congratulate us by name and saved my name until last; Mr. C called me the MVP, pitching and hitting star of the team. Yeah, I guess so, but thank God it was dimly lit, or else, people would have seen how embarrassed I felt.

As for that bike ride, travel back to my freshman or sophomore year at the Prep. I had just left some guys on Marion Avenue and East 188th Street heading north past OLM, heading across Fordham to where I lived half block away also on Marion Avenue; I paused for a minute in front of OLM's school. A very pretty blonde, name withheld, asked if she could have a ride on my English racer bicycle. I said no and left immediately. No girl was going to ride on my bike. I was fourteen or fifteen years old, and girls only would hinder my "destined" path of becoming a professional baseball player.

Back to OLM's annual bazaar. One of the guys knew some of the girls, who were also in the big room with the "wheel." We traipsed over to them, said hello, and then one of the girls, again name withheld, and by far the most beautiful of all, asked me a question by name. Odd, I thought. She knew my name and inquired, "LD, do you still have that English racer bicycle?"

I almost died on the spot. Don't you just love "inside" jokes? I do. I never followed up. Jerk!

The Hangout: H&H During College and True Friends Forever

While at Fordham University, especially in my junior and senior years, I spent many daytime free hours at a diner on the corner of Decatur Avenue and Fordham Road with four of my best friends: the future Doctor John C (PhD), a Fordham Pharmacy major, Jerry P, whom I've mentioned before, a brilliant student at Fordham College (Economics major), and two women who attended Good Counsel College in White Plains, New York: Margaret M and Margaret H, the latter we called Peg. I always called these women Margaret and Peggy, even to this day. We'd meet occasionally in the afternoon after class at the H&H—John when he wasn't working at a pharmacy and the women when they got back to the Bronx from White Plains. Jerry and I walked from classes. Being on Fordham's baseball team during the spring meant I often missed these relaxing times with my dear friends.

I've already made you aware of my knowing Jerry. I met Dr. John through a classmate of mine, Frank LoD, while we were at the Prep. I introduced JC to JP. I "jumped rope" with MM when we were at OLM while I waited for the guys to play stickball, etc. I did stop jumping rope when two of the girls' fathers called me a "sissy." Had to be a joke. I was the best ballplayer in my crowd of future cops, firemen, and attorneys. JC, GP, and LD met MH for the first time when she accompanied the other Margaret one day to the H&H. Two very cute women, yet they tolerated me and my BS sports talk. These women became very successful after college: MM with IBM and MH with Pan Am/Delta. JC and JP became very successful in the financial industry. Me? On my way to my own "stardom" in the business community, I left the corporate world to run my family's small business with my father and younger brother JJ. I didn't make much money, but my future wife Emilie and I raised two boys into manhood as gentlemen with respect for others and leading exemplary lives. At this current stage of my life, I have very few complaints. I am still waiting to hit either the lottery or someone to leave me a fortune in his/her will, although I'm really not counting on either to happen.

Dear John has passed away, but Jerry and I still converse—he in Connecticut and I in Ohio. MM and I e-mail each other, especially during the baseball season. MH and I chat often on the phone. None of us miss each other's birthday or Christmas. I've been very blessed in my life to have such close friends. Dr. John's working on building an H&H for us, but slowly, I hope, for when we five get together in Paradise.

Here's an example, a special example, of the above-named longtime friends of mine. I think you'll agree that this was quite unique.

My dear wife, Emilie Louise, was diagnosed with cancer on July 28, 2011, and passed away on August 26, 2011. Dr. John's wife, Connie, called me on August 30 and asked for the date of the funeral. I stated, "Tomorrow, August 31."

Connie said, she and John would be there, but unfortunately, they would have to be at an affair in the evening. I mentioned that door-to-door is slightly more than five hundred miles. "We'll be there" was Connie's response.

Dr J and Connie C did come to the funeral. They also arrived at the church with a few other friends of mine. John had rented a jet from White Plains, New York, to Hopkins Airport in Cleveland, Ohio, with limo service to the funeral with a return trip to White Plains. JC and CC did have to go out that evening. When JC passed into Heaven also, the "best" I could offer was to attend his funeral in Westchester County. I will also mention that JP and his wife, Linda, came to my wife's funeral, along with Emilie's best friend, Nina V, Joe Q and Garry C, and I'm sure that MM and MH would have attended if I could have reached them. My dear wife's entire family came from Virginia, at least eight of them. Also present were my sister-in-law Mary T and my son Fred and his wife Shawn. My son James played the organ throughout the service in our church. That's what my friends and family thought of Emilie Louise. I'm confident you get my point.

Failing Accounting and Going to Summer School at CCNY

God does work in mysterious ways. I failed an accounting course at Fordham, getting an F in every quiz and exam from this miserable accounting professor who had no sense of humor when I made a joke about some accounting principle he was espousing on the first day of class. I was doomed thereafter. For example, we had a test on John L. Carey's small tome *Ethical Standards of the Accounting Profession*. The only problem was that Fordham's library had only one copy, which I monopolized. I moved from one library area to another library area to read the entire book. A dear friend of mine had three Xs on the test and got a B. I had two Xs and got an F. Totally unfair, but we were taught in OLM and Fordham Prep that we just don't question authority figures. Looking back, what a load of crap!

I was working in the summer at a Cadillac General Motors warehouse and had to traipse to the subway four nights per week for that one BS semester. I took the whole accounting book at CCNY in Manhattan, not just one semester's worth. Finishing work in the warehouse, sometimes as the janitor, which was the best job in the location, I walked three blocks to the East 138th Street subway station downtown to 42nd Street, got the downtown local, and exited at the East 23rd Street station. Walking three blocks to the Bernard Baruch Building, I thought, *Not bad. Plenty of time not to be late for class.*

Enjoyed the class, and the teaching professor at City College asked me if I were taking his course to "get a head start" on my accounting requirements. I replied that "I failed the first semester." He was shocked, told me that I was the best student in his class for this accounting instruction. I was shocked hearing this, some very intelligent students at night, when one considers I failed this particular course because of a personality difference.

As it turned out, four years later, I enrolled at Baruch College (prior name: City College of New York), same building, to earn an MBA with a major in private accounting (as opposed to public accounting) at night after my daytime full-time corporate employment. Upon graduation, there were only about five private accounting majors, the majority being public accounting majors. At my exit interview, it was "suggested" that I would be placed in the PhD program with the approval of Professor Abraham B, a legend in accounting in NYC, should I be so inclined. Since I was working at Pan Am, often traveling overseas with Emilie before we had any children, and the program at night would probably take upward of five years, I really didn't know, and I said "no". Reflecting after I taught financial statement analysis for two semesters in a local four-year college, I realized I made a mistake—as big a mistake as wanting to be a major league baseball player out of college and not signing with a former New York Yankees scout. Another immature move on my part. But making mistakes and learning from them is better than just "going with the flow." I have some regrets, but doesn't everyone?

Fordham versus Columbia Baseball—Junior and Senior Years

On April 11, 1963, Gerry M threw the first no-hitter at Columbia University's Baker Field in over twenty-five years, winning 2-1. Gerry reached back often to stifle the Lions, even getting the "great" Archie R, not only a terrific baseball shortstop, but also a college football All-American talent. More on AR later. I remember it well: I "warmed up," twice ready to relieve, but there would have been a team revolution had Coach Dan R lifted Gerry. Tony G, our All-East star in senior year, hit a home run and scored the winning run. What excitement playing baseball!

The following year Columbia beat Fordham in ten innings. Archie R played an integral part in this game. With first and third in the tenth inning (AR on first base), the coach went to the mound to discuss strategy with Lenny Z, our relief pitcher. The "three comrades," Steve R, Steve P, and LD, sat as far away from the coach as possible. Everyone knew the strategy; Archie R would take a lead off first; LZ would look over and pitch home. Ralph "Dutch" S would come up throwing as AR broke for second base. AR would stop going to second, and the runner on third base would break for home plate. LZ was instructed to cut Dutch's throw off at the mound to catch the runner on third, trying to score on the throw. Simple, no? Duh! AR broke, and RS threw; the runner on third broke for home. LZ ducked! AR went back to first as our shortstop cut off the ball before it reached second base. He then threw home to catch the runner from third. LZ cut the ball off and threw the baseball to get AR going slowly back to first base, but LZ threw the ball into Columbia's dugout! Run scored, AR advanced on the errant throw, and the floodgates opened up. Columbia won big, beating the Rams 8-1. Bats and balls were tossed on our side of the field, and the three "comrades" knew it. One could hear those sitting next to the coach breathing; it was so quiet. Morale of the story: Going to college doesn't mean "school smarts" will help you in pressure situations. Playing a "child's game" like baseball doesn't help if you're a Latin scholar but inept at thinking quickly in sports.

First Date and Danbury Fair with Emilie

The Bronx Reference Center of the Public Library was the building next to our apartment building. I often used its reference facilities while in high school and college. Graduate school was no exception. One time in the latter, I needed some research and met a friend while perusing several marketing books. Sitting at a reference desk was this very attractive brunette. Contrary to my social habits, I got up and introduced myself to this woman. "Hello, I'm LD. What's your name?"

She looked up and replied, "Emilie."

For some reason, that was enough. I told my male friend to "forget about asking her out. I'm going to marry that woman with the pleasant smile and confident demeanor."

I ventured several more times to the library to try to see if she were still working there. I assumed Emilie was a college student and might just go out with me. I found out her last name and called her. Em's mother got on the phone, and I heard her tell Em that "Phil was on the phone."

Oh! Oh! Competition. I asked Emilie if she would have dinner with me and a Broadway show after her half day working on a Saturday. While I felt somewhat relieved when she said yes, who the hell was Phil? And how many Phils were there?

38

Two Saturdays later, we went to an early dinner at the Lido Riviera Restaurant, one block from the library and the only decent restaurant in my neighborhood where we could easily get a taxi downtown to Manhattan's Theater District. We went to see *The Roar of the Greasepaint—The Smell of the Crowd* (1965) with Anthony Newley (his prior hit show was *Stop the World— I Want to Get Off*), a terrific English actor. Best seats always when I went on a date; since this was so rare that I dated, I could afford the best seats. I bragged about my knowledge of the English theater that Emilie had to be impressed. There was a commotion a few rows in front of us. I suggested "some fool" was fighting for his seats. Em said nothing. The show opened with "On a Wonderful Day Like Today," and out came this fool who was not fighting beforehand for his seating. It was Anthony N! Emilie was kind enough not to comment. Our first encounter was a disaster.

I got up enough courage to ask her out again. She agreed, and I took her by subway to see a vintage Al Jolson movie. (Al Jolson was one of my favorite actors and singers, and I particularly loved his mannerisms. What a voice!) Emilie and I seemed to hit it off, and when we got back to Em's home in the North Bronx, I asked why she went out with me after that first running of the *Titanic* date. Emilie's retort was "to give me a second chance." Don't you just love a woman when she confidently says something like that?

Let's move on to the Danbury, Connecticut Fair, maybe a month and a half later, with the North Bronx Army Auxiliary Women and the bus ride. I met Em at White Plains Road and 233rd Street, and we walked to the bus taking us, her mother, and members who are her mother's friends to Danbury. At the fair, I mentioned, for the umpteenth time, that I played college baseball and would win a stuffed animal for her at one of the concession stands. The only "stuffing" down was the attendant with my several dollars because all I hit was the back wall and once the attendant himself. He gave Emilie a prize because he felt sorry for me. Screw it! Em got the stuffed animal! Emilie T never reminded me of my baseball prowess that day or any day. ELT was always positive with me and always had a perfect smile and kind words. Truly a remarkable woman! On the bus ride back to the Bronx, we played cards and enjoyed each other's company. Thank God for a second chance with this phenomenal woman!

Driver's License, Mom's '63 NOVA, and the Dead Battery

Emilie had a car and always drove us when this mode of transportation was required. I decided to get a driver's license, not because Em suggested it if we wanted to get married someday, but because I played a lot of softball for money, and if I wasn't picked up by one of the guys, I might miss the game's start and cost the team $$$!

In the spring of 1966, I finally got a driver's license. Mom tried to teach me, but our nerves were frazzled. I went to driving school for the proper instruction. It couldn't be any worse than that written test I took at the DMV on Tremont Avenue in the Bronx that year! One was given a book to read and learn/know the driving rules. Fair enough. A Spanish gentleman sat next to me and copied my answers. I passed the exam, and he failed. On a particular question, my correct answer was C, and his was A. Individual effort was required to pass the test. To this day, I'm confident that guy was still "shaking his head" about that exam. Learning to parallel park was the most difficult part of the actual driving experience. Still difficult for me to this day. I got the driver's license on my first try but detest driving. Emilie was thrilled though. Now I could chauffeur her . . . like it should always have been.

After I passed the written and driving test and had some confidence in my driving skills, I called on Emilie for a date. She wanted to go to Hunter College (at the time located in the Bronx) for a T. S. Eliot evening, and I drove. Afterward, we stopped off at a local pub—each of us one drink, I swear!— and headed to my mother's car for the drive to Emilie's home in Northern Bronx. The 1963 Chevy NOVA wouldn't start. Big trouble! I found a pay phone, called my father, and he rescued us. The battery on my mom's car was dead, and my dad gave the NOVA a boost. After profusely thanking my father, I took Emilie home and vowed never to drive mom's car again. Strong lesson: Don't drink and drive and get your own "wheels" and keep it in good working order.

Emilie Louise was a Bronx girl who went to all public schools and wanted to become a nurse but couldn't afford the tuition at a particular private college. At EC High School, Em was no. 5 in the academic "pecking order" upon graduation. I always reminded her that the difference between Catholic schools and public schools was religion. We had nuns teaching us, and public schools had a majority of Jewish educators. To this day, the Jewish people firmly believe in education.

Sadly, the tenure system allowed philistines to remain "teaching" students the ABCs but sometimes forget the ABCs themselves. Emilie became a high school Home Economics teacher and took her vocation very seriously. I can't tell you how many times Em stayed up at night preparing for the next day, week, and month with her students. There are still many teachers like Em today, but the number is dwindling.

Easter Mass and No Latin

Emilie invited me to her home for Easter dinner in 1966, with her parents' permission. I was looking forward to this occasion, but first, nine-o'clock Mass. This is the most sacred feast day in the Catholic faith, and the Mass was in English. I had never gotten used to this for several years since instituted by Rome. I guess Catholics were not attending church as the Catholic Church hierarchy thought they should. Gone were the nuns, and singing was now part of the Mass (no longer only at Christmas and Easter). Church tradition taught throughout grammar school and high school was finished. Church celebrations were also not in Latin, but the "mother tongue," in this case, English. This particular Mass was a "folk" Mass. Two singers between the ages of seventeen and twenty utilized the right side of the altar, strumming their guitars, uttering "Amen, Amen," and "Blowin' in the Wind." Complete heresy! I left the church before the Mass's end, never to return, except for weddings and funerals. Perhaps I'll return someday, when I find a good Catholic church celebrating the Mass in Latin.

I went to Em's home and had a wonderful time with her parents and two sisters, Marie and Linda. At this writing, sadly, only M is alive from this very tight-knit family. Since it was about 6:00 p.m. and still light out, Emilie and I took a walk in her neighborhood and made a date for the following Saturday, if I remember correctly. It was now that Emilie shocked me by what she told me. Emilie was not Russian Orthodox as I assumed she was as her mother was Orthodox. This was "acceptable" in the Catholic Church but not her father's religion: Lutheran. It seemed that the three girls went to St. Peter's Lutheran Church within walking distance with their father every Sunday. I told Em, "It doesn't matter to me. The Catholic Church is not the same church I knew from kindergarten."

On August 22, 1970, Emilie and LD got married in her sister's house on City Island, married by a Lutheran minister. In spite of several refusals to attend the ceremony, all came. We stayed happily married for forty-one years until this terrific woman died on August 26, 2011, not quite sixty-four years of age. We "talk" several times every day—I do the talking and she the listening this time anyway.

AMEXCO and the Department's Christmas Party

Taking a subway ride in New York City is a snap. However, this is what happened to me at Christmastime working in the corporate budget department of this national treasure. It might happen to anyone but definitely to someone like me. Every Christmastime the president of American Express made it a point to spend time with our group of nine people, a small and appreciated way of the president to thank us for the tireless work we expend for the company. Apparently, we were special for this annual occurrence. This particular visiting morning, since I was the "new guy on the block," I was assigned to travel on the subway uptown to a well-known specialty store to get utensils, some Christmas plates, and several small decorations for our small "executive" gathering for cake and coffee with Howard C, our company president.

I boarded the train at about 9:00 a.m. and headed uptown to my destination. I didn't recognize the first two subway stations. Good God! I was on the train the wrong way. I was now in Brooklyn. I had never been to Brooklyn in my life! Not even to visit Ebbets Field when I was a teenager to see one of my "heroes" Jackie Robinson (no. 42). I made a phone call to my immediate supervisor (Lou V) and explained. Laughingly, my boss told me how to transfer, and I was told I had until about 11:30 a.m. to get uptown, buy the supplies, and "get my ass back to the office," or I'll be making photocopies the rest of my life. As an aside, can anyone of you remember what the "system" was for making photocopies as late as the last few years of the 1960s? Ha! A strong light permeated the original paper and utilized ammonia to burn a facsimile through another piece of paper to get one copy. The "bearer" of this task never had to fight for a subway seat when leaving for home in rush hour. People always avoided me when I entered the subway car and "politely" gave me an isolated seat.

I arrived happily at this specialty variety store and purchased the goods with my brand new American Express (AMEXCO) credit card. (In those days, the only credit cards issued were AMEXCO's card and a Diner's Club card, authorized, I think, by First National City Bank. You know it now as Citibank.) At about 10:30 a.m., I arrived at my final destination—Wall Street station. Wait a minute—I'm in Brooklyn again! I'm going to get killed! I called my boss again and told him "I'm almost there." I arrived in twenty minutes, walked across the street to 65 Broadway, and took the elevator to our office. The budget director's secretary gave me a dirty look, took everything from me. (How could it have been so hot in the office? It was December!) The president, HC, visited and chatted with all of us, left, and my supervisor and the budget director were pleased.

I left American Express after only six months to get my "dream" job at Pan American World Airways, Inc. In hindsight, staying at AMEXCO would have boosted my career when I got my MBA. It was truly a terrific company, and you all know about the demise of Pan Am. A happy ending for working at AMEXCO was a lifelong friendship with Lew M, a St. John's grad with whom I talked often even to this day.

An interesting sidebar, while working at American Express, I'd like to share with you: I was given the assignment of accumulating the operating budgets for the upcoming year from the administration/staff departments, for example, the Controller's Office and the Personnel Department. While working with Personnel, I thought I recognized a manager from my teen years in the Bronx. In those days, I "hung" with George T and Dennis H, my closest friends. We often walked up Fordham Road to the military enlistment centers to view the uniforms soldiers wore, especially the Marine Corps. The recruiter reminded me of Dick B, the aforementioned manager in Personnel. Many years later, while married and living in Eastchester, New York, I met this familiar-looking gentleman at church. Sure enough, same guy as the other two occasions! Small world! Dick and I became good friends until he passed a few years ago.

Pan Am and the Easter House on the Mezzanine Floor

The Pan Am Building was unique because it was built over Grand Central Station. To get to the building's mezzanine floor from Grand

Central, one rode an escalator one flight. There were commercial storefronts there, and a short walk north put you on 45th Street between Vanderbilt and Park Avenues. At Easter time, a small bungalow house was stationed closer to 45th Street surrounded by flowers—very imposing sight to brighten up one's day. I often enjoyed walking past this scene at lunchtime for two to three years when, all of a sudden, it disappeared completely. Since the Pan Am Building was immaculately kept, it's really no wonder what transpired. Building maintenance removed the bungalow and floral arrangement because homeless people used the house as a residence over the years and often littered the flower garden with you name it. Well, it was a pleasant sight while it lasted.

Paris, France, with Brother JJ in 1969

In 1969, I took my first Pan Am overseas trip with Brother JJ. We were on the Boeing 707 to Paris, France, and ordered two drinks, when my name and several others were called by the flight attendant to leave the aircraft. The flight was overbooked and non-managers must relinquish their seats. Completely embarrassed, about ten of us left the plane. I apologized to my brother, and we sat for something to eat in an airport café before heading home. To my surprise, Pan Am needed another plane in Paris, and as we had several flight attendants (called stewardesses in those days) who also disembarked, we were set to leave JFK on another plane with maybe half-hour delayed departure. The plane was just about empty. We "parked ourselves" wherever we wished to sit. Total comfort!

Arriving in Paris was now an adventure: two brothers with no French, only Latin, German, Ancient Greek, and some Russian. Latin and the latter two compliments of JJ; Latin and German, my languages. We arrived at a seedy hotel I picked— pictures usually present a better idea of the accommodations. JJ wanted his own room, so I obliged him. As we had arrived in the morning, we met at about 7:00 p.m. to "explore" Paris. We stopped at a pub and ordered two drinks. The bartender poured me my scotch, but JJ couldn't get his "Seven and Seven." Right, the bartender couldn't speak English. We left that dump, went to see a *Laurel and Hardy* movie in French, and traveled to Harry's American Bar, a staple in several cities in Europe at this time, for hamburgers and a few drinks. Since "it's a small world," the first guy I chatted with was from the Bronx.

In one to two hours, my brother and I went back to the hotel for the night. I only found out the next morning that Brother JJ didn't go to bed; he went to the Crazy Horse, a cabaret several blocks from our hotel. Lucky he wasn't killed.

We visited the Louvre, Napoleon's Tomb, and the Eiffel Tower. We stood on the corner where the Bastille had been, and I envisioned the French Revolution. What a terrific city! I asked JJ if he wanted to go home—we only had a long weekend here anyway. Brother JJ had football practice, and I wanted to see the Baltimore Orioles crush the New York Mets in the World Series. We got home in fine condition, only for me to see the Mets take the next four games to win the championship. JJ bought something for his girlfriend, Anita G, his future wife. I purchased something for our mother and, of course, some Joy perfume and two silk scarves in tax-free airport shops for my girlfriend, Emilie Louise, my future wife. It was a cheap trip, total cost less than dinner and a Broadway show in Manhattan, except for the presents. After all, I worked for the most famous airline ever and did get some reductions in charges. FYI: Brother Jim and I went on our honeymoons, in different years, to Paris and acted as "tour guides" for our wives. Emilie was the only person who spoke French. Some tour guide I would become for my new wife!

THE EARLY 1970S

Married Life with Emilie

To wit, we were married in the house of Emilie's sister in City Island (Bronx) on Saturday, August 22, 1970, and left for Paris the next day, Sunday. We arrived in Paris early Monday morning. Passed the cheap hotel where JJ and I stayed— looking back, he and I got a roundabout tour by the cabbie from Orly Airport to our hotel. It only took thirty minutes from Orly to our hotel (Intercontinental Hotel owned by Pan Am) while passing the hotel where JJ and I had stayed taking about twenty minutes. Ripped off by the French! The only problem was that since we got married on a Saturday and the flight left on Sunday, arriving Monday, I made the Intercontinental reservation also for Sunday. I forgot we arrive the next day from the reservation when one leaves at night. My Uncle Pat T met us at JFK and got us first-class accommodations through his Pan Am contacts. First class to Paris—what a honeymoon! I was so glad for my dear wife. She longed to always travel to France, but the cost was too prohibitive for Em to even dream of Paris. I got it for her.

Panic enveloped me. When I talked to the concierge and the desk clerk, I was told there were no available rooms. My booking was for Sunday, and when we didn't appear, the room was given to another party. After pleading that I was on my honeymoon and worked for Pan Am in NYC, they'd see "what they could do." Yeah, sure! I remembered Paris and how JJ and I were treated. Besides, after all, it was August. Em was sitting patiently with our luggage, and when I approached her, she asked, "What was wrong?"

I replied that the room was being cleaned since we arrived so early. I was told to come back in about three hours. We went around the corner, in view of the Louvre, upstairs into an English pub. Emilie knew her new husband like the back of her hand. "Okay, Louie, what did you do or didn't do?"

I explained the situation, and there was no panic on her part. As usual, a woman knows best and handles a crisis better than a man—at least this man. We got a lovely room in this five-star hotel and spent six wonderful days in Paris and vicinity.

The highlight to me, other than being with Emilie, was our guided tour of the Louvre. Upon entering this amazing "wonder of the world," we were "greeted" by *Venus de Milo*, she of the head and no arms. There was a huge painting by Jacques-Louis David of the *Coronation of Napoleon Emperor* with Pope Pius VII present to give the ceremony credibility. In fact, Napoleon crowned himself. Of course, *Mona Lisa* was the most viewed and admired. Looking at this tiny portrait from any angle, one would swear that she was smiling at you. Another facet of the genius of Leonardo da Vinci. My favorite was the *Slaughtered Ox* by the greatest artist of them all: the Dutch Rembrandt van Rijn. This was a slab of meat that the tour guide stated, "Rembrandt wanted to prove that 'art is art,' no matter what is painted!" Here it hangs in the Louvre.

My dear wife was in her glory and held my arm throughout our stay in the City of Lights. I'm grateful she did hold my hand. I didn't want to get lost when I only spoke a "dead" language, Latin, and the hated German tongue. We did not go to the Crazy Horse!

Pan Am—Juan Trippe and "The" Charles Lindbergh

The genius of the Pan Am Building in NYC, now named the Met Life Building, was the fact that it was built over Grand Central Station. It was opened in 1963, and I was fortunate to start work for that mighty international airline in 1968. It was a dream come true for me. An uncle of mine worked for Pan American World Airways, Inc. and often brought me geography books when I was in elementary school. Even though an entrance to the NY Public Library's Bronx Reference Center was less than two hundred feet from my apartment's front door, I utilized my Uncle Pat T's Pan Am books for class work. Plan B was for me, someday, to work for Pan Am. I did turn down an internal auditor's job offered by Pan Am and took a budgeting position at American Express until the right fit for me was available at Pan Am. It came that April 1968, working for the corporate budget department, although I was in the analytical section of the group, much more interesting work assignments.

One afternoon after lunch, a coworker of mine, Gerry M, and I were ready to take the elevator to the 49th floor, our floor. The executives were domiciled on the 45th or 46th. Upon entering the elevator and stepping to the rear, we noticed that Juan Trippe, the legendary grandfather and Godfather of commercial aviation in the United States, was on the elevator with Harold Gray, the current president. Oh! Oh! There standing across from GM and me was the man who made the nonstop flight over the Atlantic Ocean in 1927, Charles Lindbergh. Yes, the "Great Man" himself standing so erect and powerful-looking without saying a word. I froze for a second and then blurted out to my coworker, "There's a lot of talent on this elevator."

No idea what made me say that. Well, Mr. Trippe stared that icy stare of his at me as if to inquire why I would be even breathing in his presence. My immediate thought was what he could do to me. Couldn't shoot me, only fire me. I now thought my comment funny, and if I were fired, so what? I'll find another job. Lindbergh said to Trippe and Gray that "we'd never have an SST in this country."

But Mr. T said nothing in response, and the three of them exited on the executive floor.

When GM and I arrived at our office, Gerry went to his cubicle, and I went into the office of our immediate supervisor, Jim M. JM was working on an SST airplane request from senior management. I suggested that I was talking with Chuck L, and he mentioned that we'd never have an SST airplane in this county. JM asked why I never told him that I knew Chuck L. I responded that "I don't like to throw names around."

Then GM came into JM's office and said, "Who do you think was on the elevator with us? Charles L!"

I wanted to kill my friend and coworker, but JM just looked at me and said nothing. I shrugged and went sheepishly to my desk to work on an aircraft leasing request from the sales department, one of my special duties. What a terrific place of employment!

Getting Living Quarters and Our First New Year's Eve, December 31, 1970

Looking for living quarters was tedious and time-consuming. I thought Emilie and I had found a nice apartment in the Allerton Avenue section of the Bronx, but the superintendent wanted a small down payment—read: a small bribe—to "get" us this apartment. While it was close to the parkway for Em to drive to work in Yonkers and a three-block walk to the elevated subway for me, I wasn't about to give any money to a building super like this guy. Ironically, someone Em knew from working in the Public Library had a neighbor in Mount Vernon, just over the Bronx border, who was looking for a tenant in his two-family house. We jumped at the opportunity: close to Emilie's mother and close to an East Side subway and better for me than the West Side subway off Allerton Avenue. No problem for Em to get to work either. We had a wonderful owner and ideal location. And Em was allowed to have her dog with her.

As mentioned prior to this episode, in August, Em and I went to Paris, France, on our honeymoon. Our first New Year's Eve together was "around the corner." Where would Emilie like to go? Not "we," it seemed! Emilie went to Hawaii (via Pan Am, thank you) with her mother to visit family, and I spent part of the eve with sister-in-law, Linda, then to Danny K's apartment in the Bronx with Danny and his wife. Footnote to this: I was Danny's best man, and Danny was in my wedding party, so I was a welcomed guest as he was painting their apartment, but only until I arrived to have some New Year's Eve beer. Shortly after midnight, I got a cab (how, at that time?) to my parents' home off Fordham Road and Marion Avenue and spent the night. The next morning I couldn't believe the snow. I walked five minutes to the bus stop on Webster Avenue (Bronx), and zero was running. Fortunately, a cabbie was parked on Webster, and I offered double to get me at least to the Bronx border. Done, and I walked two blocks to our home and Emilie's dog, fed the "darling" pet, took a shower, and when dry, took the dog for a walk.

Our landlord and his son knocked on the door and brought me "tons" of chicken and pasta. Knowing my wife was not home, they showered me with food and beverage. They must have thought it "funny" that our first New Year's as a married couple would find me a "bachelor." I didn't mind being by myself. Emilie didn't want her mother to travel alone, so I insisted that Em fly on my Pan Am discounted fare to see her cousin. After all, Emilie had many years in the future to travel with her husband, which we did for only two more years because I left my "dream" career, because of the airline's sagging finances. Louie Dubois and dearest wife did visit Rio, Tokyo, and many places in Europe, so no complaints. I would do anything for my wife because she also put me first in everything—everything! I was blessed to have this woman in my life.

Injured Playing Softball and That Night's Dinner Party

Saturday morning and another July softball game with George C and Danny K. But this Saturday was going to be special. My two friends were coming to dinner at our apartment. Emilie was going to cook something special. But first, another softball game on blacktop with a team of friends—a team that belied the athleticism of several of us.

In the third inning of a tight game—we usually lost these types—we were ahead by one run. A short pop fly to right got me moving from my first base position and racing toward the foul line. Where was the damn right fielder, Pete M? Well, I found him, when he crashed into my left arm. I hit my mouth with such force that I broke my two front teeth when I bit myself on the flesh just above my left knuckles. Blood was oozing from my mouth and between my left wrist and knuckles. I definitely found the right fielder. And I just missed holding on to the pop fly.

Well, no one could take me to the hospital, save a nice guy on the far end of the two playing fields. Without saying a word to me as I compressed the "future" stitching-needed cut in the emergency room at a local Bronx hospital, my Good Samaritan left me to a nurse taking an X-ray and an intern to follow shortly fixing the wound, bandaging my left hand, and getting me a cab home to Mount Vernon, where Emilie and I lived. My dear wife couldn't believe this could happen to her "jock" husband, but I allayed her worries with "Don't worry. I can still use my left hand to write when I go to work Monday. I'm fine." That afternoon I went to a dentist—who became a lifelong family friend—who put two temporaries in my mouth. None would be the wiser, except for the purple color taking over my pale white skin and knuckles. Little did I ever dream of what was to befall me when I arrived at Pan American the next Monday morning. Later for Monday.

That night, at the dinner table with my two closest teammates and their wives, I asked, "How'd we do?"

George stated that "we were tied going into the sixth inning."

One doesn't have to be a brain surgeon to know we lost—again. George's wife, Barbara, tore into George for not driving me to the hospital. Danny's wife, Kathy, just stared at her husband. Most of us know what that means. Emilie told everyone, "The dessert's on the way, so let's enjoy the rest of the evening."

I mentioned that I would have done the same as George and Danny. "We had a shot to win the game. Leaving would have given us only seven players and a forfeit," George rationalized. As did I.

Women just don't understand athletes and their "silly" games.

Oh! The meal and dessert were perfect, as usual, with my wife's careful preparation, cooking, and presentation. This from a Home Economics teacher who married a gourmet hamburger eater.

That Fateful Monday at Pan American World Airways, Inc.

What did happen that Monday morning after my softball collision? Here goes: I arrived at the office that morning and answered several questions about my appearance (bandaged left hand, discolored knuckles, front teeth temporarily replaced). I received a call to meet Pan Am's corporate counsel in the conference room (the floor I don't remember) because there was a scheduled meeting with about ten other airlines to, as the lawyer stated, have only a "brainstorming" session, get a better return on investment (ROI) for use of our aircraft for the Military Airlift Command (MAC) for transporting troops back and forth for the Vietnam War. As Pan Am was the largest subscriber to this program, Mr. Elihu S was the chairperson for the meeting. Why me? My immediate supervisor, JM, was on vacation, and the VP was attending his son's First Holy Communion. Since I was responsible for the P&Ls for this "moneymaker," I was "it." The attorney had no idea who I was, and I had never met him.

After a few introductions, a member of an all-cargo carrier and I had a discussion regarding a ROI on sole-owned aircraft. As the largest subscriber to MAC, Pan Am had much more to gain with the inclusion of leased airplanes to the return formula. I told the audience we were to utilize a "constructive ownership" approach—passenger and cargo aircraft owned and leased—to what we wanted from the federal government for our services. After I explained this methodology, several of the carriers present were so impressed by my ad hoc dissertation that I received two home telephone calls with job offers. Sorry, but going every day to JFK from Westchester was out of the question. Mr. S relayed his impression to my supervisors concerning my performance that shortly thereafter, there was a department-rearranged organization chart, and I was promoted to manager with three guys reporting to me. But most important to me was the added flight benefits one receives as a manager. Worth thousands of dollars flying free and no IRS worries! Ironic how events come into play when one cares about one's duty to a company and one doesn't call in "sick." How's that working out in the work environment today, I wonder.

Two Embarrassing Episodes Later (Much Later) in Life

I left the airline industry in 1972 for a future with two other corporations. Offered a return to Pan Am about four years later as a staff vice president and two other opportunities, I chose to work closely with my family, namely my father and Brother JJ. Let me share one with the latter and a "sports pat-on-the-back" from teammates much later than college days past.

1. While standing in line with Emilie at the New York Athletic Club, waiting for a dinner table, I noticed that Gene Rayburn of *Match Game* fame was waiting patiently right in front of me. I said hello, and Mr. R returned the pleasantry. I said, "How soon they forget!" Mr. Rayburn just glanced at me. "Mr. R, Louie Dubois from so and so."
   "Louie, Louie Dubois! How nice to see you! How's Brother JJ?" Spoken so loudly, people in nearby rows jerked their heads and wondered who Louie Dubois was. They looked at me like I was the celebrity, not Gene Rayburn. I smiled.
2. Much later I played slo-pitch (sissy!) softball in Greenwich, Connecticut, with older guys, myself included. In the championship game, I made seven to eight plays at first base and got four hits. Two weeks later at our gathering in a Queens, New York restaurant to celebrate the victory, Emilie and I were sitting at the bar with Jon J and his wife. Two of our teammates arrived

and passing us, said that "we would not have won without your playing first base."

No one ever said that to me before. Other "comments," but not something as complimentary. I had a great night!

EPILOGUE

Really, whatever happened to this guy? As already mentioned, he had an opportunity to sign with the Baltimore Orioles right out of Fordham University but chose graduate school. Had that head Metropolitan New York baseball scout stayed with the NY Yankees, LD would have signed with the NYY. Baltimore? No way! Had I played baseball for a living, I wouldn't have met Emilie. I feel, honestly, that without Emilie Louise, I would have been a nomad wandering in the desert. This woman gave me structure and proper direction in life. As the saying goes, "The proof of the pudding is in the eating."

Louie married Emilie, seen here gazing out a window in her wedding dress, looking like she just posed for a Johannes Vermeer painting.

Emilie was a remarkable woman who made "this guy" a better person; a woman bereft of any unkind thoughts or words toward another human being, a woman who inspired her husband of forty-one years (until her passing in 2011) to attend church regularly, a woman who raised two boys to become gentlemen and respectful of others, a woman who put her family always before herself, a woman who entered Paradise all too soon.

Quod Erat Demonstrandum: I married a terrific woman and mother. I have two admirable sons. And I still go to church! As Frank Sinatra sang, "I did it My Way!" Again, capiche? You should be so lucky!

"Love is eternal like the first smile, hug, and kiss from the person most dear to you . . . that person other than your mother!" (FCF)

Signed, Louie Dubois, AMDG

Printed in the United States
by Baker & Taylor Publisher Services